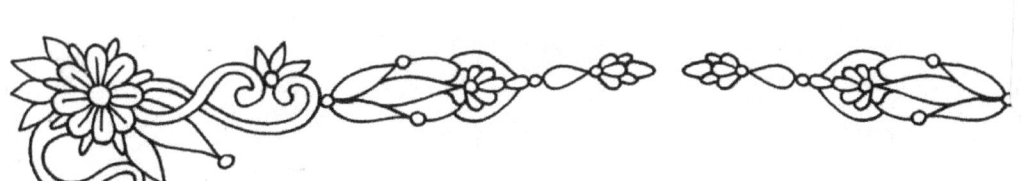

Olga Goloveshkina

Adult Coloring book

ENCHANTED
HORSES

Olya's SketchBook 1

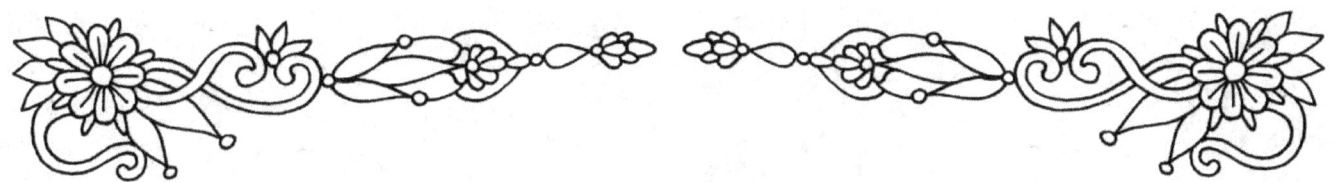

Happy coloring

Thank you for choosing my coloring book!

Olya :)

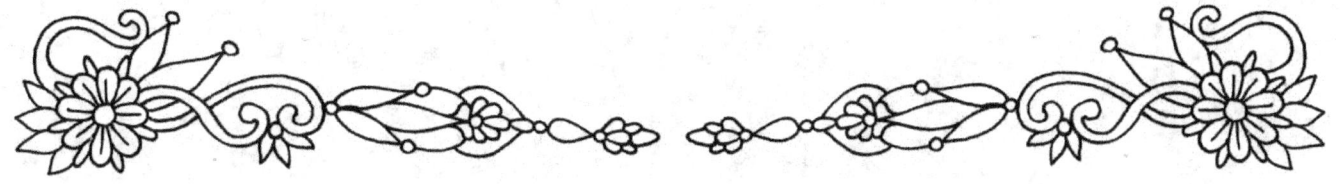

This book belongs to

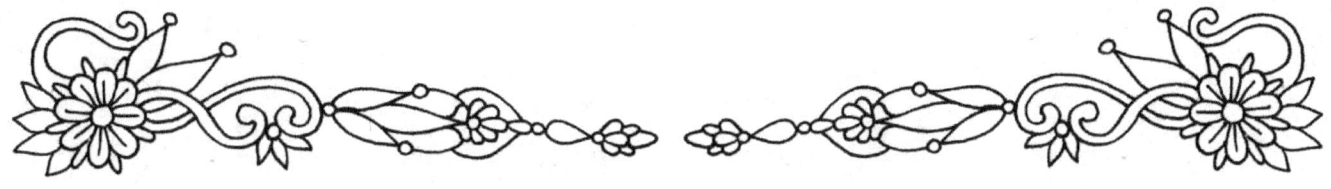

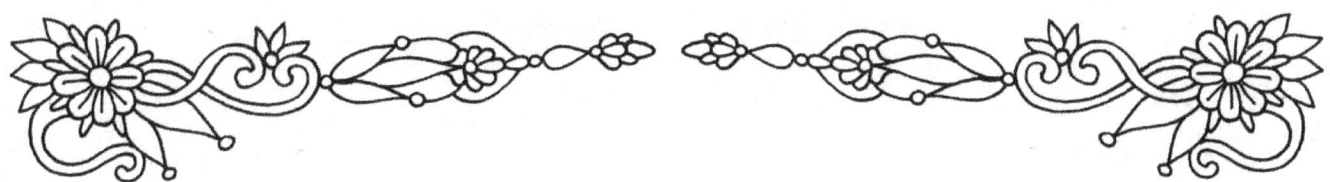

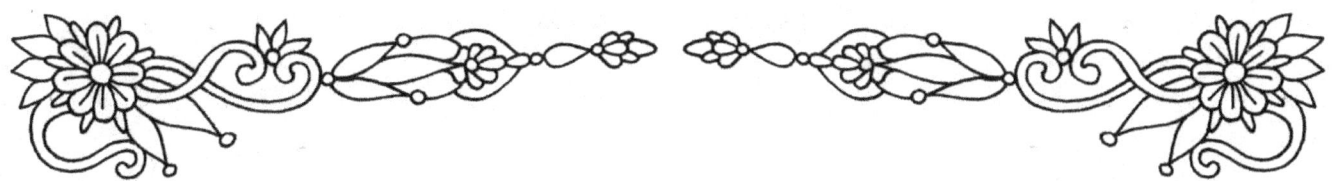

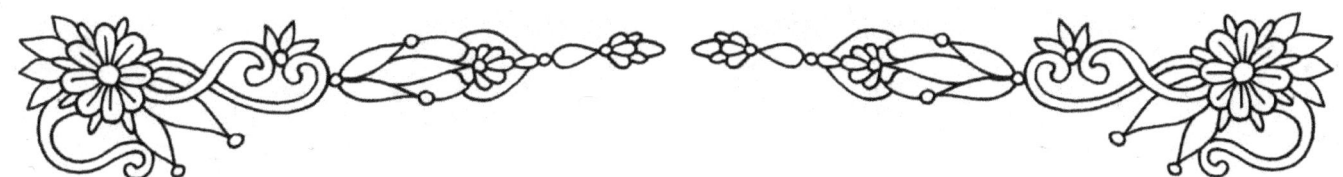

KEEP CALM AND LOVE HORSES

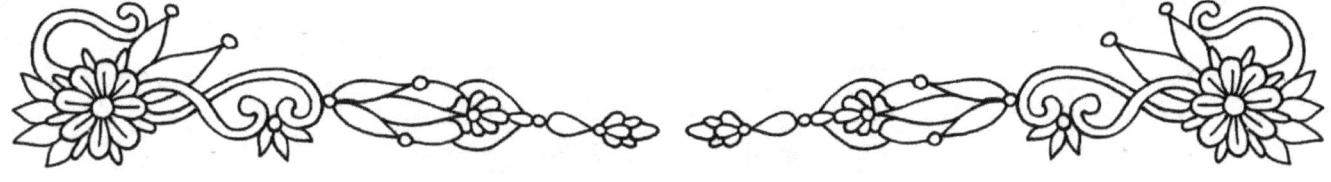

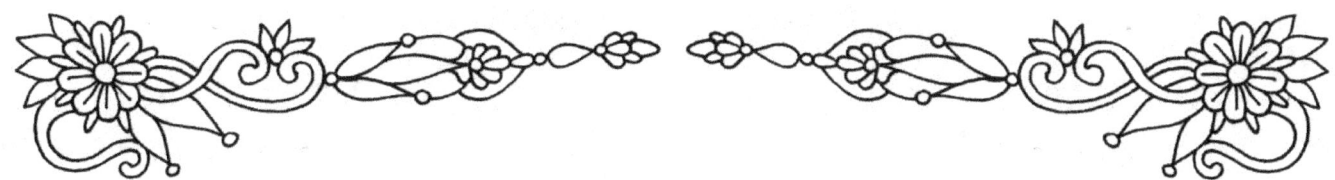

I Love Horses and Ponies

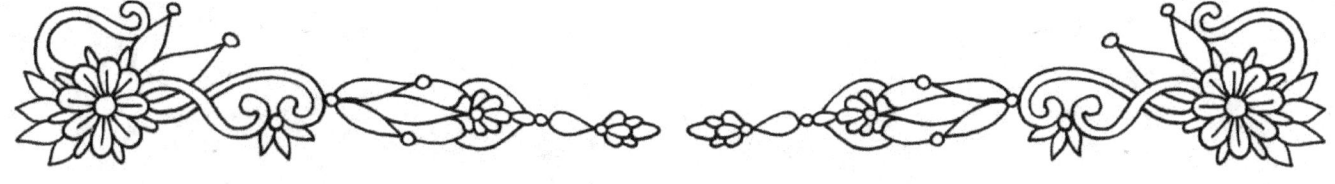

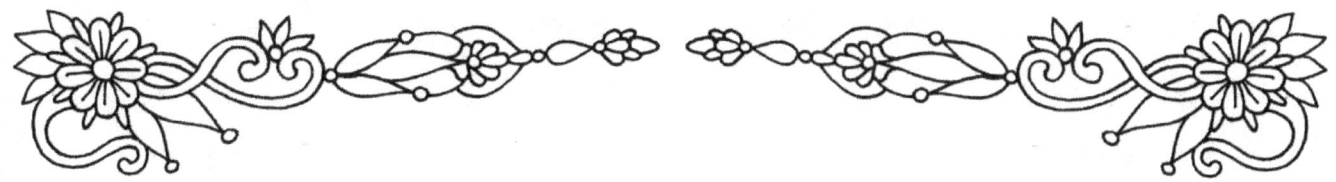

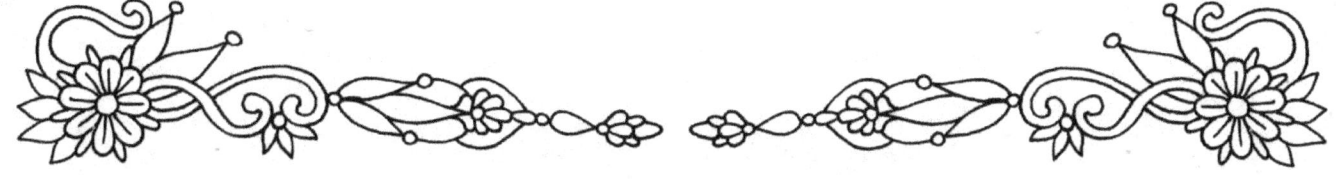

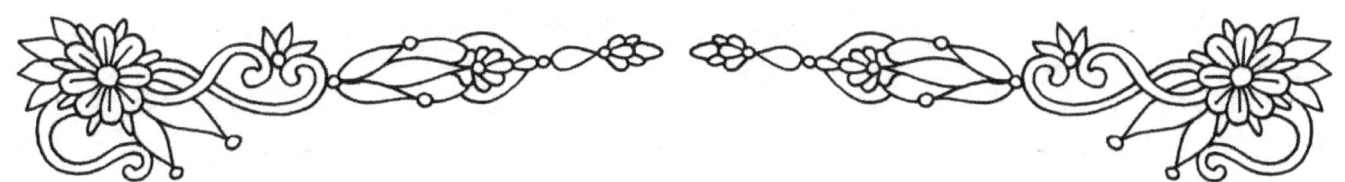

I love horses

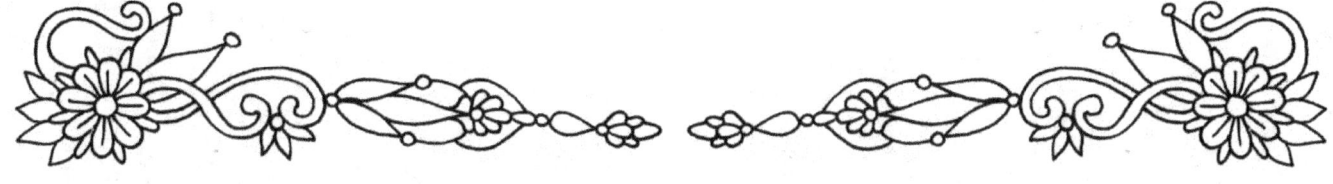

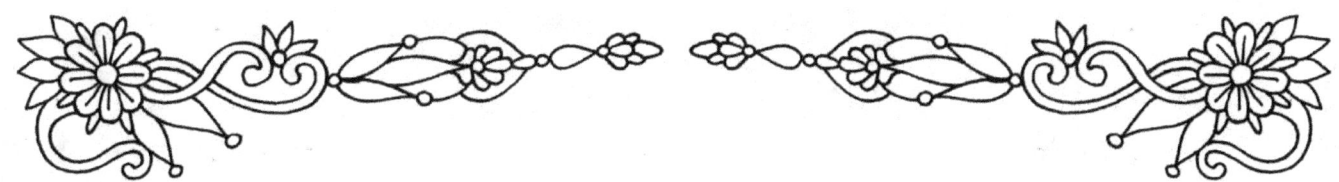

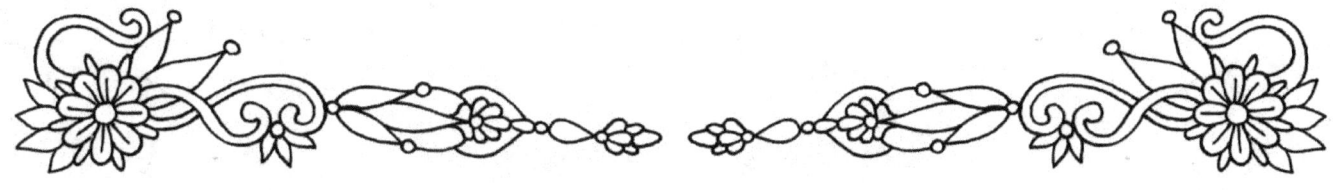

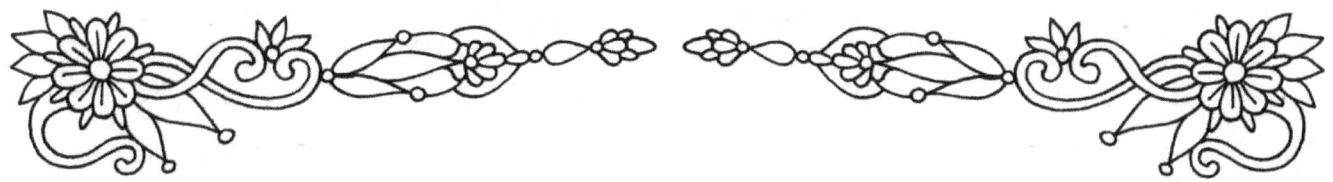

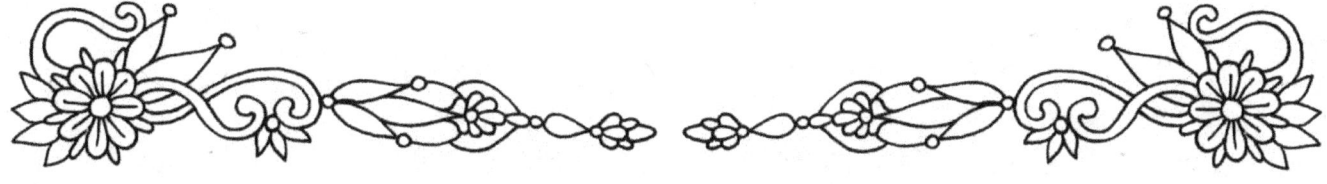

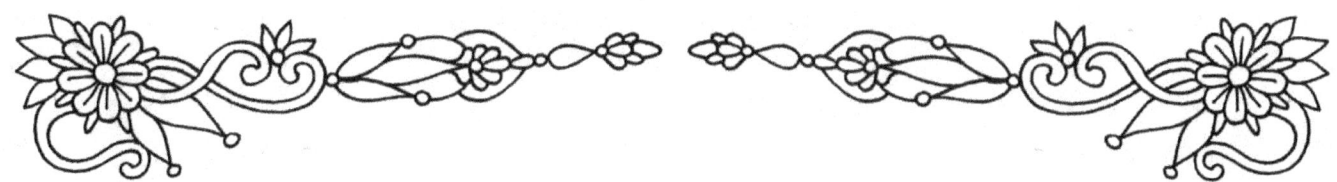

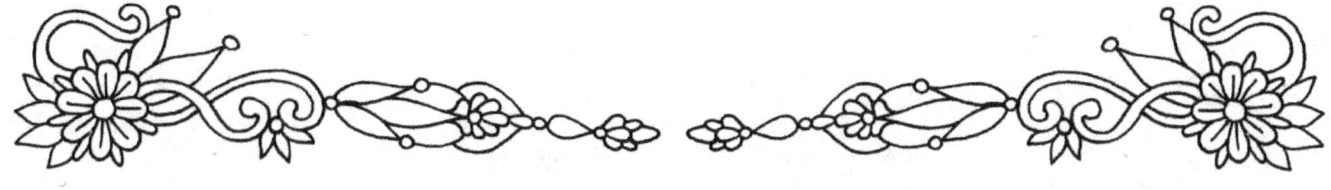

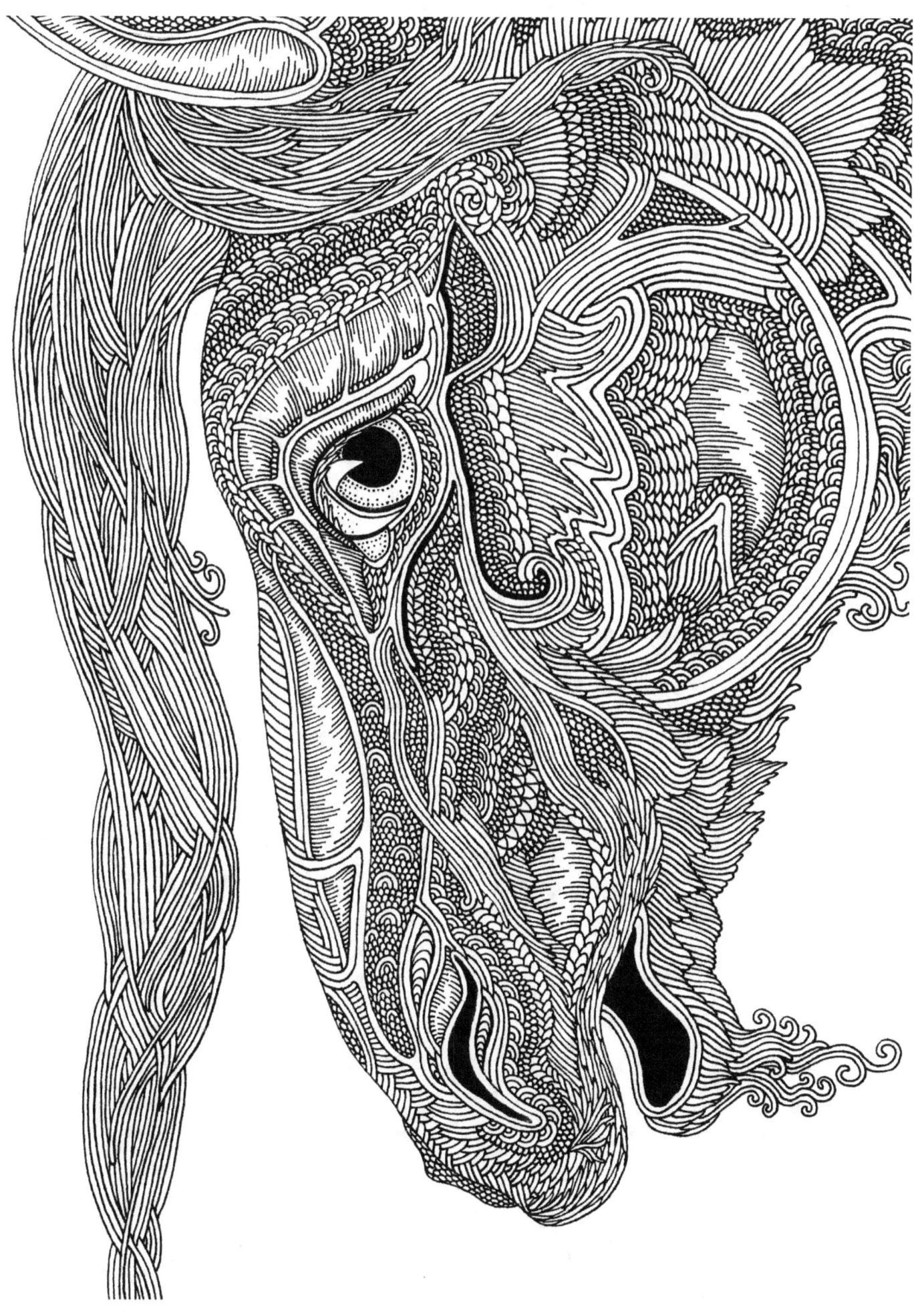

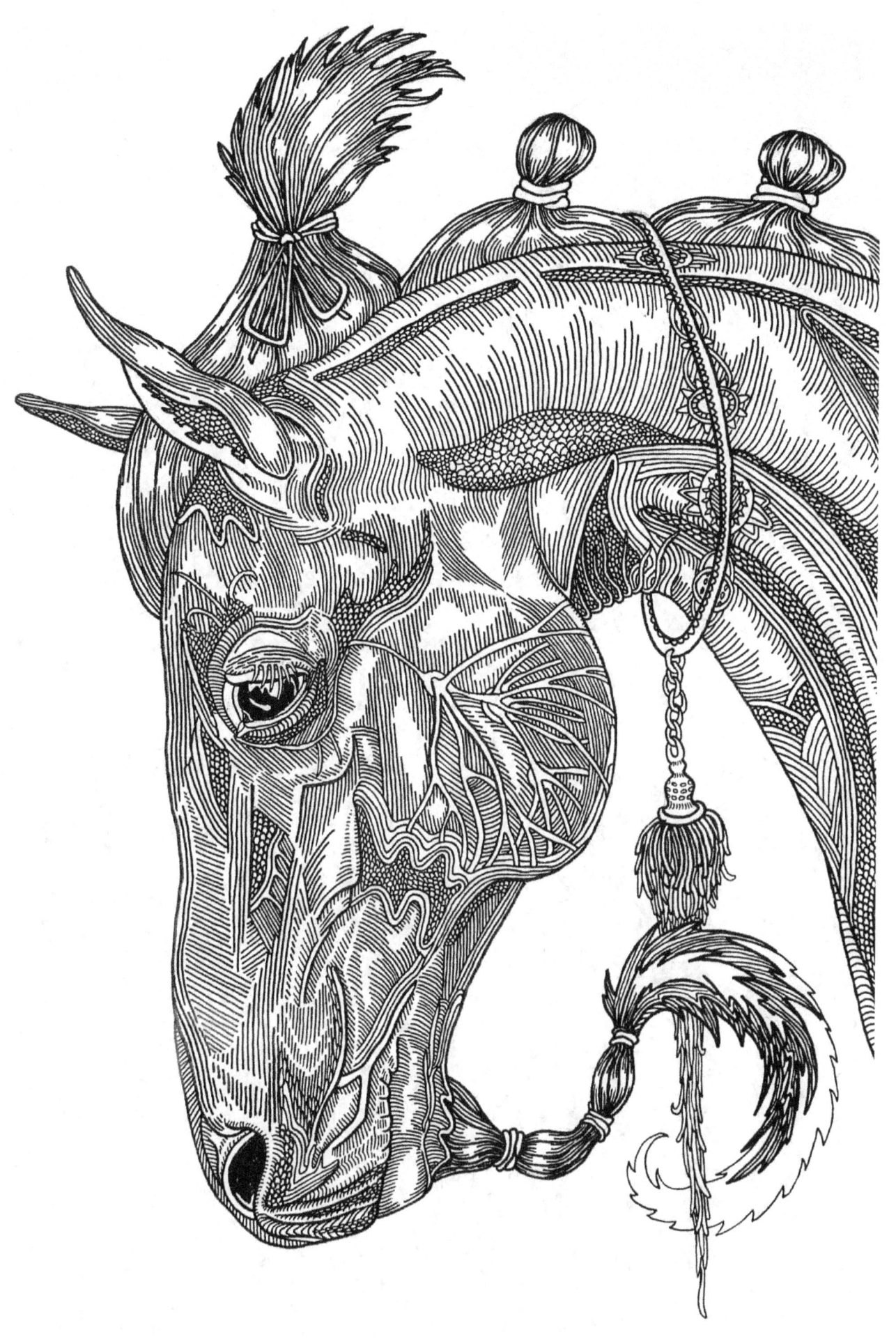

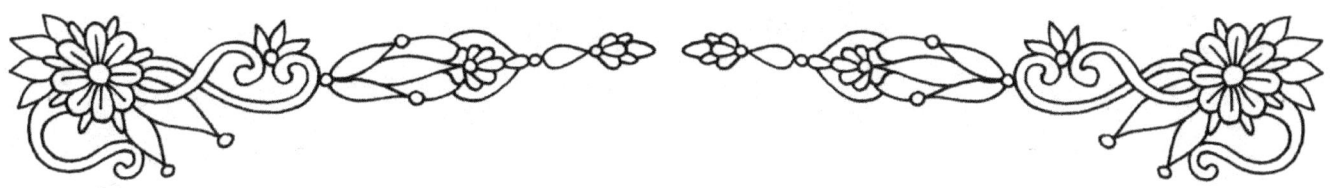

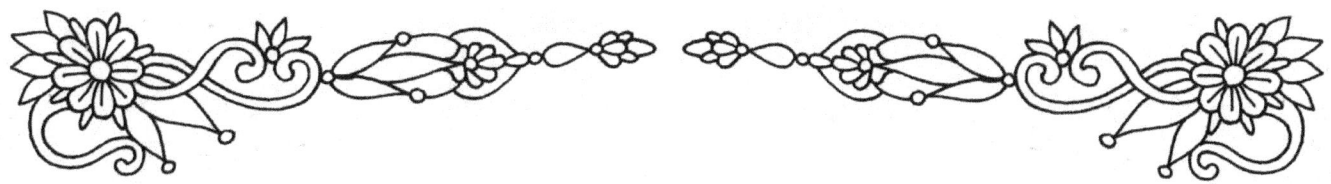

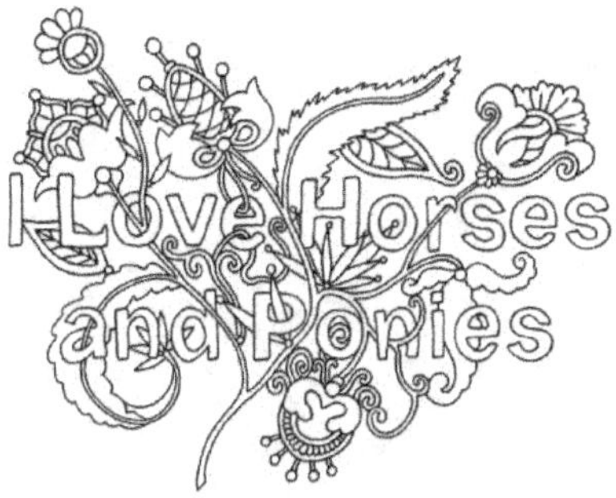
I Love Horses
and Ponies

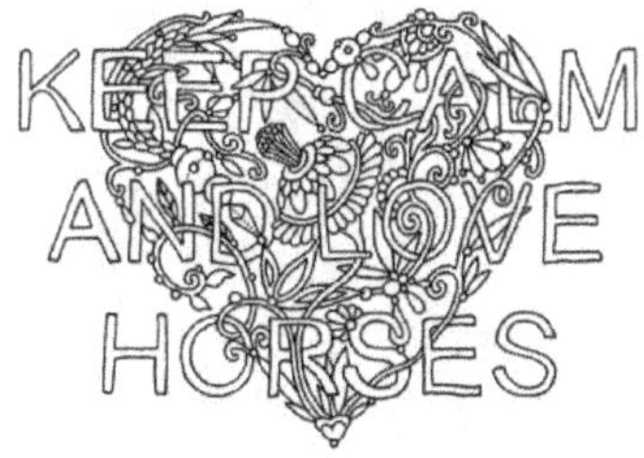
KEEP CALM
AND LOVE
HORSES

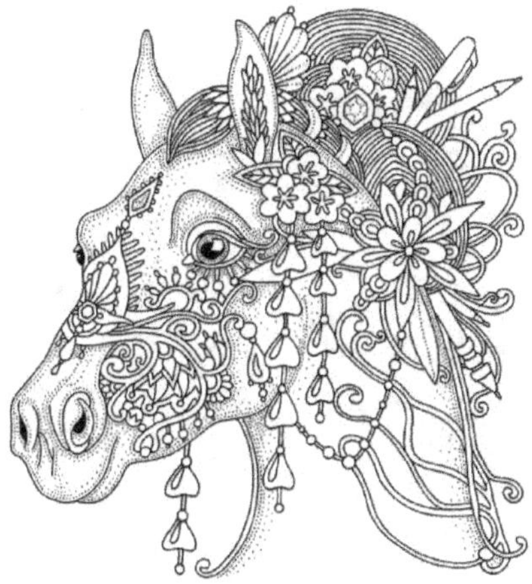

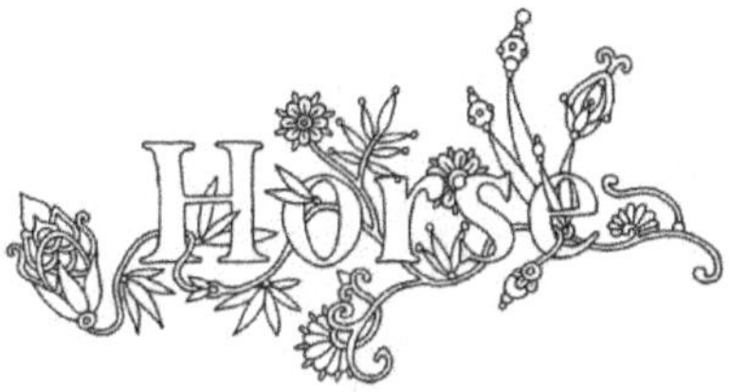
Horse

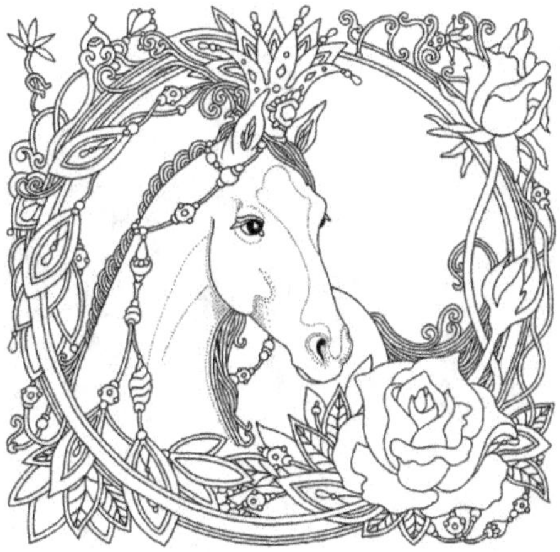

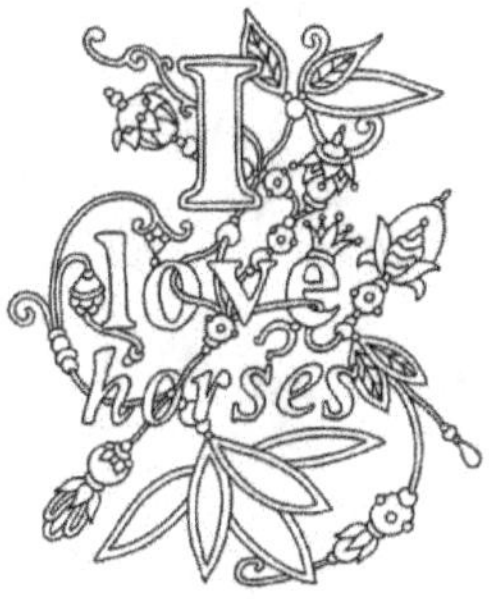
I
love
horses

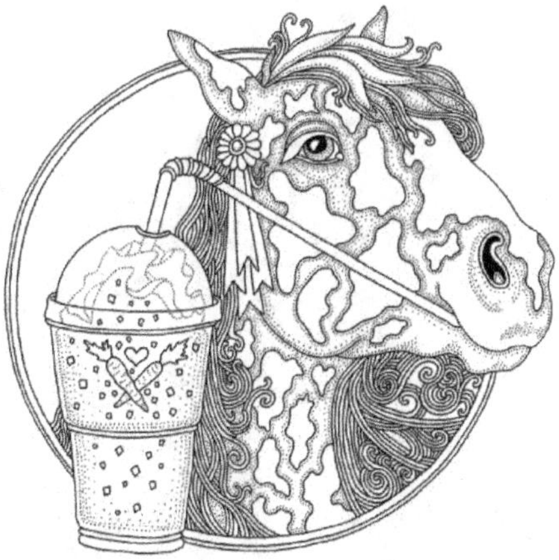

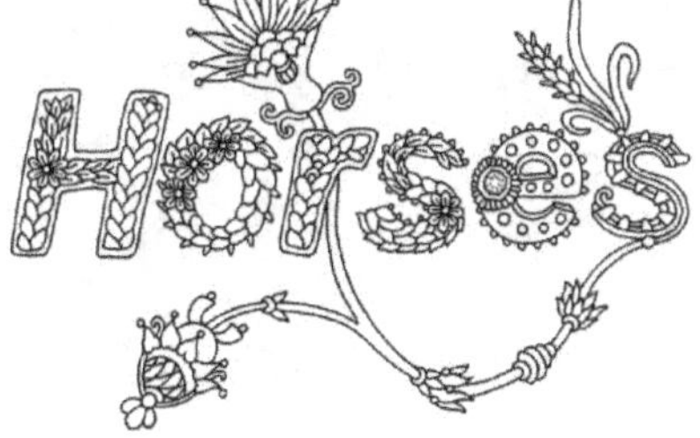
Horses

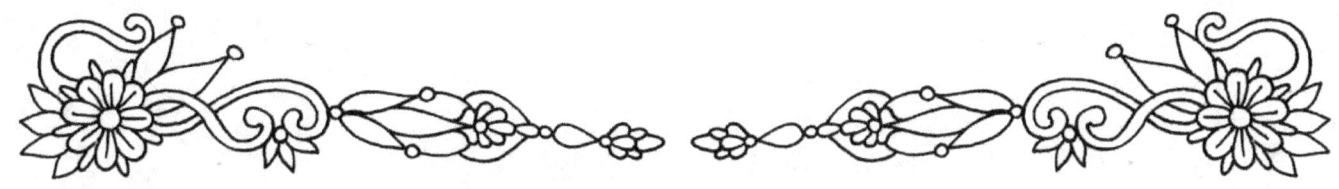

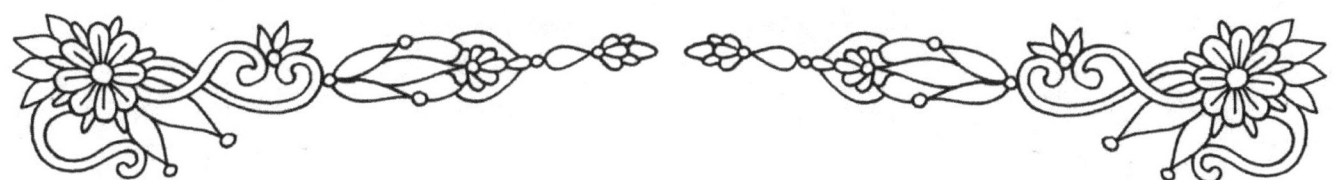

www.ingramcontent.com/pod-product-compliance
Lightning Source LLC
Chambersburg PA
CBHW081834280526

45789CB00007B/2451